THE LAST VALOIS
1515–90

COSTUME OF THE WESTERN WORLD

Edited by James Laver

THE TUDORS TO LOUIS XIII

EARLY TUDOR, *by James Laver*

THE LAST VALOIS, *by André Blum*

ELIZABETHAN AND JACOBEAN, *by Graham Reynolds*

THE DOMINANCE OF SPAIN, *by Brian Reade*

THE GREAT AGE OF HOLLAND, *by Frithjof van Thienen*

EARLY BOURBON, *by André Blum*

Each uniform with this book
With 8 Plates in Colour
and Many in Monochrome

COSTUME OF THE WESTERN WORLD

THE LAST VALOIS
1515—90

by

ANDRÉ BLUM

Conservator at The Louvre Museum

Translated from the French
by D. I. Wilton

GEORGE G. HARRAP AND COMPANY LTD
LONDON SYDNEY TORONTO BOMBAY

First published 1951
by GEORGE G. HARRAP *&* CO. LTD
182 High Holborn, London, W. C. 1
Copyright. All rights reserved

*This edition is not to be sold in
the United States of America or its
Dependencies.*

Intercontinental Publishing Company, Amsterdam
Text printed by H. Veenman & Zonen, Wageningen
Colour and monochrome plates printed by Vada, Wageningen
Printed in the Netherlands

THE LAST VALOIS

1515–90

THE EXPRESSION 'Renaissance costume' is often used to describe the dress which was worn in France in the sixteenth century, but the term is an ambiguous one, for it is applied in Italy to that of the Quattrocento. It is as well, before indicating its salient features, to point out that we are concerned here with the fashions which were current in the reigns of the last Valois kings—that is to say, not under the dynasty beginning with Philip VI (1328–50) and ending with Charles VIII and Louis XII (1498–1515), but under the Valois-Orléans-Angoulême branch, of whom Francis I was the first representative and Henri III the last.

At first glance it seems illogical to ascribe so much importance to the influence of the monarchs on their times and to divide fashions into reigns. It may also be objected that there is little point in recapitulating the dates of the four kings who ruled in this period—Francis I from 1515 to 1547, Henri II from 1547 to 1559, Charles IX from 1560 to 1574 (his elder brother Francis II, who died at the age of sixteen, having reigned for only a year), and, finally, Henri III from 1574 to 1589. But these dates are essential for our purpose, because they mark the different stages in the evolution of costume in the sixteenth century. Here, ready at hand, is a convenient method of classifying the successive changes which occurred in dress, which were due not so much to the influence of the kings themselves as to the changing tastes of their Courts.

How far do the tastes of the sixteenth century differ from those of the late Middle Ages, and from those of the princes who at the beginning of the Italian wars first began to import Italian modes into France?

At the end of the Middle Ages women's costumes and headdresses were remarkable for their extravagant proportions and their sumptuousness. A fifteenth-century canon, Guillaume Coquillart, who was a poet, makes fun of their gowns furred with ermine "with fifteen flutes," their silk and silver girdles, their satin *cottes*, their laced bodices, their fillets, their tall hats, and their shoes with high soles. A preacher of the day, the Franciscan monk Michel Menot, was no less scathing in his sermons attacking the rich fabrics of their dresses and their adornments.

At the time of Louis XII and Anne of Brittany a reaction set in against these exaggerated fashions. A poem by Olivier de la Marche entitled *Le Triomphe des dames*, or *Le Parement et le triomphe des dames*, written at the beginning of this reign, describes in great detail the various items of feminine dress which marked the new trend: the linen

5

chemise, the simple *cotte*, the lacing drawing the gown together, the cloth hose, the girdle, the 'honest' coif, the gorget, the garters, the ribbons, the shoes, the gloves—in a word, a whole ensemble instinct with virtue. Thus the so-called Italian gowns did not borrow from Italy, as they were to do later, an extraordinary wealth of ornaments and jewels.

Here we see one of the principal features of the change in manners which had taken place between the reigns of Francis I and Henri III. From the time of the reception given by Francis I to Henry VIII of England at the Field of the Cloth of Gold to the fêtes organized by Henri III luxury and magnificence had been unrestrained. Velvets and silks enriched with gold or silver embroidery, lace ruffs and ruffles, a profusion of jewellery and gems—everything pointed to unbridled extravagance, which the series of sumptuary decrees enacted between 1532 and 1583 was powerless to check.

This is borne out by the testimony of many contemporary manuscripts. In the first place we have the *Relations* of Venetian ambassadors like Jérôme Lippomano, who in 1577 remarks that

> the changes of costume customary in France call for considerable expenditure on cloth of gold, wool, and silk. A man about Court is not esteemed rich unless he has twenty-five to thirty suits of clothes in different styles, and he must change them every day.

In the same year we find Claude Haton writing in his *Mémoires*:

> Despite the prohibitions and penalties laid down in the decree of 1577, the new gentlemen and *damoiselles* have shown no intention of reducing their state or discarding their new velvets and habits, and I have never heard of their paying the thousand-écus fine.

Brantôme's *Mémoires* also speak of the increasing richness displayed in women's gowns from the reign of Henri II to the end of the century. Though on the death of Henri II Diane de Poitiers dressed "with modesty" and the ladies of her Court followed her example and took to austerity, Brantôme describes, later, other mourning styles for women which were more ostentatious and less decorous.

When Henri Estienne in his *Dialogues du nouveau langage françois italianisé* refers to Henri III's police order of November 21, 1577, restricting the use of precious fabrics, he makes this reflexion:

> Never have people been at such pains to tell from the habit where the highest honours belong, for to-day we see not only gentlemen but *galefretiers* [people of low extraction] wearing broideries and other adornments which were formerly the prerogative of princes, or at least of the most noble lords.

It follows from this passage that visible signs of richness of attire were the monopoly of the wealthy, and that if the *bourgeoisie* ventured to infringe the decrees they were usurping the rights of their betters. The pictorial records of the sixteenth century consist almost exclusively of portraits of *gentilshommes* and noble ladies. We have to accept the convention that the fashions of this period were those of the Court, and are thus obliged to disregard those of the other classes of society.

What strikes us most about men's dress is the contrast between the first half of the sixteenth century, when the doublet was loose at the neck and sleeves were puffed, and the second half, when the head was buried in a cambric collar or a pleated ruff, surmounting a doublet high at the neck, tight at the waist, tilted forward so as to form a hump, and with sleeves as close-fitting as the nether-hose. The trunk-hose, instead of being short, reached below the knee. These elegancies of the late Valois period were much admired; they probably came from Spain, where this stiff and starched effect was in great favour, even for children.

Spanish influence was likewise reflected in women's gowns in the adoption of the *quilted bodice*, which was also known as the 'Spanish body.' It was a sort of busked corset shaped like an elongated cone, giving a slim-waisted appearance made still more pronounced by contrast with the *vertugadin*, or farthingale, a large roll of padding placed under the skirt to accentuate its width. The farthingale, which had been extremely popular in the reign of Henri III and sprang from the *vertugade*, or hoopskirt, of the time of Francis I, was also probably of Spanish origin, if we go by the presumed derivation of this word from the Spanish word *verdugo* ('green rod'). To this device for making the gown stand out we must add an appendage borrowed from Italy—the ruff of pleated lace, which grew taller and taller until it enveloped the head. If we felt tempted to caricature this accoutrement we might compare it to a surrealist composition featuring a dish, a lump of sugar, and a balloon.

Even the pencil of a Dumonstier or the brush of a Corneille de Lyon or a Clouet fails to bring these costumes completely to life. The fine portraits we have of them, notwithstanding their realism and the extremely careful rendering of the materials and the adornments, are somewhat static. We shall find, however, when we have learned all they have to teach us, that we can reawaken life and movement in these illustrious lords and great ladies who under the last Valois kings, in spite of foreign wars and religious and political strife, had sufficient leisure to devote to the details of their toilet to avoid the danger of being behind the fashion, to dress according to the latest mode, and to launch an uninterrupted succession of new styles.

Costume in the Reign of Francis I

The masculine costume of this reign was different from what it had been under Charles VIII and Louis XII. Sleeves, instead of being slit, were slashed and puffed. The doublet was cut low at the neck, as in Clouet's portrait of Francis I (Plate 17); it was made of some precious fabric, cloth of gold or silver, velvet, satin, or damask. The hose were rather long, embroidered, dagged at the top and bottom, and of different colours. The *braguette* was conspicuous. The cloak was short, with open sleeves.

Rabelais has described the salient features of these costumes in a passage concerning the Abbey of Thélème. This is what he says:

The men were dressed in the mode of the day; hose, the lower part of *étamet* or serge faced with scarlet, white, or black migraine, the upper part of velvet, of the same or nearly the same, broidered

7

and dagged to suit their fancy, the doublet of cloth of gold or silver, velvet, satin, damask or taffeta in the same colours, dagged, with broidery and accoutrements to match. Aiguillettes of silk in the same colours, the gold tags well enamelled, says and *chamarres* of cloth of gold, cloth of silver and velvet galore; the gowns as rich as those of the ladies; silken girdles the same colour as the doublet, and each with his fine sword at his side, the hilt gilded, the scabbard of velvet of the same colour as the hose, the tip of gold and goldsmith's work, the dagger likewise; the cap of black velvet garnished with an abundance of gold rings and buttons, the white feather prettily strewn with gold spangles.

To these we must add the overgarments, such as the cassock, which differed from the *chamarre* Rabelais speaks of, the former being a long, wide vest, while the latter had hanging sleeves.

On their heads men wore either a velvet or cloth cap, or, more often, a low-crowned felt or satin hat (Plate 1). The turned-up brim was kept in place by a sort of brooch known as an *affiquet*.

The *Comptes des Bâtiments du Roi*, published by Léon de Laborde, give a list of various articles of dress ordered by Francis I between 1532 and 1538 for the ladies and gentlemen of his Court. Among these items we find numerous lengths of black velvet, black and white taffeta, linen of gold or silver, crimson satin, Dutch chemises, muffs, and *cannetilles*. To import these precious fabrics he authorized the Genoese merchant Emmanuel Riccio in 1538, notwithstanding all the existing embargoes, to ship to the kingdom of France 2347 pieces of velvet of all colours and silks of Genoese manufacture without paying the duty of two écus a piece.

When his consort, Eleanor of Austria, had made her State entry into Paris on March 16, 1530, and into Bordeaux on July 27 of the same year, Francis had had gowns made in the Spanish style for her ladies-in-waiting; these figure in the same collection of accounts. As for the Queen's dress, this is described in a report of the ceremonies: "Round her neck was a fine carcanet, precious beyond measure."

The books recording the royal expenditure do not tell us anything about women's costume. The chief innovation of the period was the *vertugade*, or farthingale, a sort of petticoat of coarse stiff linen covered by a taffeta skirt, very wide in the lower part and shaped like a cone; it was attached at the waist to the edge of the *vasquine*, a sleeveless, very tight-fitting whaleboned jacket (Plates 36 and 45).

Rabelais tells us all about these fashions:

> The ladies wore scarlet or migraine hose, the said hose reaching just three finger-lengths above the knee; and the border made of some fine broidery or openwork. The garters were the same colour as the bracelets and crossed above and below the knee. The shoes, pumps or pantofles, of crimson, red or violet velvet, were cut out in the shape of lobsters' beards. Above the chemise they wore a handsome *vasquine* made of some fine silken camlet, and over this *vasquine* came the farthingale of taffeta, white, red, etc. Above this, the *cotte* of silvered taffeta of broidery of fine gold wrought with needlework.... The gowns, according to the season, were of linen of gold interwoven with silver, red satin, etc. Sometimes in summer instead of gowns they wore fine *marlottes* of the said stuffs, or Moorish bernouses. And always a cluster of fine feathers matching the colour of the muffs, well garnished with gold spangles.
>
> The *patenôtres* rings, *jazerines* and *carcanets* were of precious stones.

Some of these terms require explanation: the *marlotte* was a cloak shorter than the gown and open in front; the *bernous* was like the marlotte, but without sleeves; the *carcanets* were jewels, the *patenôtres* pendants of goldsmith's work, and the *jazerines* gold chains worn on the bodice.

As for women's headdresses, Marot in his *Dialogue de deux amoureux* mentions "the cap like a bandage" (Plate 6). Others were the *espagnole*, a velvet toque ornamented with a feather, and the *tusque*, a lawn coif secured on the forehead and temples by ornaments in goldsmith's work.

Cauls garnished with pearls were also fashionable (Plate 34); later the pearls were interspersed with gold ribbons with fleurettes.

In military costume uniform now began to make its appearance. Every regiment had to display the distinctive colours of its ensign or captain. Archers and cross-bowmen had been replaced by pikemen, halberdiers, and, after the battle of Pavia, harquebussiers, as we see them in the bas-reliefs on the tomb of Francis I in the Abbey of Saint-Denis. Helmets were supplanted by the flat-brimmed *cabassets* or the *morions* with their pronounced crests (Plate 5) and the *burgonets* which recall the helms of antiquity. The body was encased in a *corslet*, a sort of cuirass at the bottom of which was a bell called a *tonnelet*. There was also a suit of armour imitating that worn by the German foot-soldiers, known as a *hallecret*.

Fashion under Henri II

As we have seen, Henri II, like Francis I, prohibited the wearing of garments made of silk and velvet or trimmed with gold and silver, thereby earning the praise of Ronsard. But this monarch's influence was perceptible only in the use of black and sombre colours. In his portrait by Clouet he is in black and white traced with gold. The doublet has also undergone a transformation. It is no longer open at the neck as in the preceding reign, but has an upstanding collar rising above the top of the shirt, turned over, and ornamented with lace and embroidery (Plate 9). The doublet has basques concealing the upper part of the trunk-hose and slit in the middle of the front to show the *braguette*. Sleeves are puffed and tight at the wrists. The trunk-hose look like rather short, baggy trousers. Stockings are made of silk, *estame*—i.e., woollen yarn—or *tricot*, a new word of uncertain origin. The other appurtenances of this costume are the camisole, or under-garment, the cassock, and the sleeveless say (Plates 9, 27, and 40).

Blaise de Montluc recalls in his *Commentaires* that in 1555 he wore crimson velvet breeches covered with gold lace and a doublet and shirt of silk with a 'swallowed,' or rather deep, collar. He also speaks of a velvet tunic trimmed with silver trefoil.

As for the women, they wore the farthingale and the *vasquine*, but we now witness the appearance of the quilted bodice (Plates 13, 14, and 22), a sort of corset supported in front of the chest by ivory or steel busks, and the standing ruff (Plates 8, 11, and 14).

In the contemporary accounts of royal entries, such as that celebrated at Lyon on

September 18, 1548, the clothes worn by the King and Queen, Henri II and Catherine de' Medici, are only very briefly mentioned, but there is a lengthy description of the costumes worn by the corporations and the guards, who are referred to as "children of the town." What strike us in these processions are the colours of the velvets and the silks, the graceful plumes, especially those of the captains, and, in general, the splendour of the armour and the morions, which are chased and gilded (Plate 7).

The only evidence we possess as to the dress worn during the short reign of Francis II, which lasted barely a year, is that of Régnier de la Planche, who, in his *Histoire de l'estat de France*, mentions as a feature peculiar to 1559 the long cloaks and the wide trunk-hose which permitted arms to be concealed beneath them and were banned by the King's Privy Council.

Dress at the Time of Charles IX

The trunk-hose of this reign were of various types, Italian, Flemish, or Spanish. Pockets were invented, and in them were placed the ovoid, round, or flat watches recently produced at Nuremberg. An order of 1563 decreed that hose were not to measure more than two-thirds of an ell round or to be trimmed with fur; the order was not enforced, however.

Stockings were either long or short, and either attached to the trunk-hose by *aiguillettes* or secured below the knee by garters. The space between the stocking and the trunk-hose was occupied by *genouillères*, or knee-pieces, which later became *canions* (Plates 42 and 67).

Cloaks were of various kinds—the collarless cape, the cape with a standing or turned-down collar, and the long ample *reître*. The cassock was a cape with a slit allowing the sleeves of the doublet to pass through (Plate 27).

Men's headgear (Plates 16, 20, and 26) usually consisted of a velvet toque ornamented with precious stones and white feathers, or a narrow-brimmed felt hat.

Women continued to favour the farthingale and the quilted bodice. Gowns became fuller to give a small-waisted effect (Plate 23). They were trimmed at the neck with a cape-collar, from which issued a large collar of pleated cambric known as a 'ruff' because of its resemblance to the bird's ruff. It was pleated and goffered, and held in place by a necklace known as a *carcanet* (Plates 18, 19, 24, 29, 34, and 35); it had been imported from Italy by Catherine de' Medici. Gowns had leg-of-mutton sleeves (Plate 52), or tight-fitting sleeves with puffs or burlets at the top (Plates 23 and 56).

In *Le bref et sommaire Recueil de ce qui a été fait et de l'Ordre tenu à la joyeuse et triomphante Entrée du Roy Charles IX en sa bonne Ville et Cité de Paris, mardi le 6 mars 1572*, the King's costume is described in these words:

> The king was clad in a suit of white armour curiously polished and enriched, adorned above with a say of cloth of silver garnished with *cannetilles*. His hat, also of linen of silver, was bordered by a band set with many precious stones, and its feathers studded with fine pearls.

As for the costume worn by Elizabeth of Austria, Charles IX's wife, this is described in a pamphlet entitled *C'est l'Ordre qui a été tenu au Couronnement de la Reine Elisabeth, le 25 mars 1571*:

> In the morning the Queen was in her chamber clad in a bodice, a surcoat of ermine and a mantle, with head ornaments and other royal habiliments. And her mantle was of perse velvet broidered with fleurs-de-lis and lined with ermine, the train of the said mantle being seven ells long. Her head ornament was garnished with precious stones, her aforesaid bodice also of perse velvet covered with fleurs-de-lis, and her surcoat decorated with large diamonds, rubies, and emeralds.

In the portraits which Clouet has bequeathed us of Charles IX and Elizabeth of Austria (Plates 27 and 57) he shows them in more everyday costume, shorn of ceremonial pomp; but he has not omitted to indicate the sumptuousness of the jewellery and the gems. Even where women's headgear is concerned we know from the testimony of the ambassadors that the velvet cap, or *escoffion*, was a coif consisting of a network of gold or silk ribbon, often ornamented with precious stones. Another simpler headdress, made famous by Catherine de' Medici, was the widow's cap, with a point on the forehead and a veil with or without looped bows falling behind the head (Plates 2, 31, and 47).

In military equipment soldiers, who had been armed with pistols in the time of Henri II, now began to use pronged *harquebusses* called muskets. They still wore *morions* and *burgonets* on their heads, but the *cuisses* were now replaced by *tasses*, and the cuirass covered by the cassock, the *mandilion*, and, finally, by the scarf, a long piece of folded material, generally red or white. The pikemen still wore the brassarded corslet, which, like the *morion*, was chased and gilded.

Henri III and Splendour of Attire

Henri III is said to have been fond of perfumes and cosmetics, ear-rings, velvet or satin muffs lined with fur—in fact, a whole range of modes formerly reserved for the use of women. But, owing to his unpopularity with many of the aristocratic families, they did not all attempt to imitate him in his eccentricities. We must make a distinction between those who were known as his 'Mignons' and the rest of the nobility. There were two ways of dressing, one in the manner of the King, the other following a trend which was practically international, the elements being contributed by countries as far apart as Spain and Poland.

This mode became widespread in France about 1580; it consisted of new versions of the upper-stock and the nether-stock. The appearance of the short, baggy trunk-hose (Plate 40) coincided with that of others which were narrow, close-fitting, gathered, and reaching to the knee (Plate 42). These two forms, which existed separately, were sometimes combined. The wide trunks hugged the hips down to the middle of the thighs and then turned into something resembling trouser-legs, finishing in silk stockings, which were already embryo *canions*. Several collections of water-colours which have been preserved at the Louvre and at the Bibliothèque Nationale in Paris indicate that the *grands seigneurs* thought highly of this type of costume, which they wore frequently in town and also for various kinds of sports (Plates 45 and 67).

These trunk-hose, which were often equipped with *lodiers*, thick strips of satin or velvet from the waist to the middle of the leg, were called *grègues* ('breeches'), a term probably derived from the Spanish *griga* (Plates 56 and 64), and not of Gascon origin.

One of the most novel features of the doublet was that it was fitted in front with a *plastron* in the form of a hump (Plate 64), known as the 'paunch,' stuffed with horse-hair, wool, and tow. This paunch, which had been imported from Poland, tilted the waist and the belt forward, and was used in the army as a means of protection against bullets. This is shown in an engraving by Goltzius representing a standard-bearer (Plate 62).

Cloaks were either capes, secured on the left shoulder and reaching to the hips (Plate 54), or long mantles known as *reîtres*.

Shoes were sometimes in the Grecian style and sometimes in that of Savoy, either wide or narrow, short or long. They often had a shape like a heel at either end, or one single heel in the centre.

Shirt collars were no longer invariably turned down, and often consisted of ruffs starched with a mixture containing rice flour. These ruffs were high, pleated or fluted collars, an idea of which can be obtained from the picture in the Louvre of a ball at the Court of Henri III (Plate 52).

The headdress of the period was a cap with an *aigrette*, decorated in front with jewels, a beret, or a broad-brimmed hat. The hair, supported at the back by a circlet, was powdered.

The effeminacy of Henri III and his associates, the Mignons, was ridiculed by many of their contemporaries, some of whom, like Agrippa d'Aubigné, were more than ordinarily virulent. He wondered as he beheld his sovereign whether he was looking at "a woman king or a man queen."

A book by Thomas Artus, *Description de l'Isle des Hermaphrodites*, describes one of the Mignons at his toilet. He is handed first a pair of puffed breeches with long silk stockings attached, then a pair of narrow shoes, after which a valet offers him a shirt of cut-work with an embroidered collar. Next, another valet presents him with a doublet, shaped and close-fitting, heavily padded, buttoning up with difficulty, and adorned with large lace ruffles and a shoulder-cape, showing the white shirt beneath. His hat covers only the top of his head, thus allowing the hair decorated with precious stones to be seen. He wears long ear-rings, and chains of pearls on his arm and falling down the peascod-bellied doublet.

Another writer, Blaise de Vigenère, in a book published in 1583 containing annotations to a French translation of Livy's *Decades*, makes fun of the strange figures cut by two gentlemen encountered at a game of tennis. The first gentleman's doublet is skin-tight; that of his companion is ample and dagged, with a heavily stuffed peascod-belly and long sleeves. One wears an *obelisk* hat, the other a flat *sombrero*. As for

12

their cloaks, one is long, and the other very short, allowing the head to pass through a ruff with organ-pipe pleats.

Henri Estienne's *Dialogues du nouveau langage françois italianisé* tells the same story, in 1578, of the variety of styles worn by men. According to this writer, gentlemen were dressed after the style of Spaniards, Italians, Teutons, Flemings, Hungarians, or Poles. There was a vogue for long cloaks, short cloaks, and *reîtres* falling to the heels.

The Venetian ambassador to France, Jérôme Lippomano, records in 1577 that in masculine dress new fashions followed one another daily or even hourly. He adds that though the shape of the garments varied, the manner of wearing them was not less extravagant on that account. "The cloak is always draped over a sword and hanging loose on the other side, one sleeve of the doublet open all the way down and the other buttoned up."

Jérôme Lippomano's picture of women's dress is no less interesting:

> Frenchwomen have very slender waists; they like to puff out their gowns from the waist down with paniers and farthingales and other devices, which gives still greater elegance to the contour.... Over the chemise they wear a corset or jacket they call a *quilted bodice* [Plates 35, 61, 64, 66, and 68] which lends added lightness and slenderness to the figure. It fastens at the back. Their throat and shoulders are covered with very fine gauze veils; head, neck and arms are adorned with jewels.

This device for tight-lacing, consisting of a quilted bodice in imitation of the peascod-bellied doublet, had been imported from Spain and was known as a 'Spanish body.' "To have a really Spagnolized body," says Montaigne, "what tortures they endure, all girded and pinched in, with whalebone sticking into their ribs."

The farthingale was shaped like a drum (Plates 43, 52, 67, 69, and 70) and accentuated the elongated cone shape of the quilted bodice. Sleeves were puffed from top to bottom and had turned-down cuffs trimmed with lace. Gowns were open at the neck, which was framed in wide, pleated ruffs, sometimes spreading out like fans, supported by brasswire under-props. 'Wings' of some light fabric (Plates 36 and 65) were often attached to the back of the gown. Footgear consisted of mules, pumps, or Italian shoes.

Among the women most conspicuous for the ostentation of their dress pride of place must be given to Marguerite of Valois, sister of Henri III and the future wife of Henry of Navarre (afterwards Henri IV); in 1578 Brantôme praises "a gown of linen of silver, in the Bolognese style," she wore on a journey to Cognac. She herself describes with approval "the Spanish habiliment of Marguerite, Countess de Ligne, covered with linen of gold and silver, with diamond broidery and buttons."

But it was at the fêtes and the royal entries that the most sumptuous costumes of all were displayed. The two pictures, at the Louvre and Versailles (Plates 50, 51, 52, and 64), representing a ball in the reign of Henri III give us an idea of their magnificence. Fancy costume, which was popular chiefly under Louis XIII, is already to be seen in 1582 in Balthazar de Beaujoyeulx's *Ballet comique de la Royne, faict aux nopces de M. le duc de Joyeuse*, where Circe appears in a gown of gold veiled with silver tissue and silk, her neck and arms enriched with precious stones and pearls.

13

Under the last of the Valois kings changes were made in military uniform. The plate-armour, the accoutrements, the cuirass, and the corslet were condemned by the great captains as being too heavy. The fashionable breast-plate was preferred to the old unwieldy means of protection. Only the pikemen still continued in the old tradition. Changes were also being introduced in arms, and we shall shortly see carabineers with their pistols and their carbines, musketeers on foot (Plate 58), and harquebussiers armed with wheel-lock harquebusses in the cavalry.

Conclusion

This survey of costume in France in the times of the Valois kings gives us some idea of French Renaissance fashions. Headed for simplicity at the beginning of the century, they veered rapidly in the direction of eccentricity. There was a repetition of the attacks once made on the modes of the end of the Middle Ages. The similarity of the charges is sufficiently illustrated by a comparison of the epigrams contained in the *Spécule des pécheurs* with a work by Antoine Estienne written in 1585 entitled *Remonstrance charitable aux dames et damoyselles de France*. The author of this book attacks the different styles of headgear, the *passefilons*, the *attifets*, the *escoffions*, the masks, the capes, the ruffs, the pleats, the busks, the velvet, satin, damask, and taffeta gowns, open at the neck and enriched with a superabundance of embroidery, the exaggerated far-thingales, the calecons, the *hacketons*, the silk nether-hose, the chains, the rings, the bracelets, and the necklaces.

A number of other contemporary writers ridicule these "inept and intolerable modes." Thus Montaigne tells us that changes in fashion are so many that styles once disdained find favour again and novelties are discarded in the space of a few years with incredible fickleness and frivolity.

THE ILLUSTRATIONS

It will be a simple matter to follow the evolution of men's and women's dress through the reigns of Francis I, Henri II, Charles IX, and Henri III if we define and illumine the principal features in which changes occurred.

Let us consider, for instance, the portrait of Francis I ascribed to Jean Clouet at the Louvre (Plate 17). He wears a low-necked doublet with slashed sleeves fitting tightly at the wrists, covered by an overgarment, or *chamarre*.

When we compare with it François Clouet's portrait of Henri II at the Louvre (Plate 9) we find that fashions have already changed. The doublet has become an overgarment, is no longer *décolleté*, and has a sort of jacket separating it from the shirt. The neck has a turned-down collar.

In the portrait of Charles IX by the same artist, also at the Louvre, the turned-down collar will have been exchanged for a pleated one. We notice, too, that whereas Henri II wore slung over his doublet a cape with bands of stuff *traced*—i.e., stitched with gold threads—Charles IX wears a cassock with open sleeves (Plate 27).

When we come to Henri III the pleated collar will have given place to the ruff (Plates 43, 55, and 56). The doublet will be busked and equipped with a stuffed plastron known as a peascod-belly (Plate 62). The sleeves will be puffed, the shoulder-cape short and secured on the left shoulder (Plate 54).

There have also been some changes in the trunk-hose. These were short and puffed under Francis I; they remained unchanged under Henri II and Charles IX, but in the reign of Henri III they became close-fitting, with a *culot* over the hips (Plate 40), and lengthened until they reached to the knee (Plate 56).

The nether-hose of the reign of Francis I were of different colours. In the reign of Henri II they ceased to be parti-coloured (Plate 9); at the time of Charles IX they were worn very long and tight and either fastened to the trunk-hose with *aiguillettes* or secured below the knee by garters. Under Henri III they were, in fact, clinging stockings made of wool or silk (Plates 54, 55, and 64).

Men's headgear at the time of Francis I consisted of a shallow-crowned felt, velvet, or satin beret ornamented with white ostrich feathers (Plate 1). The brim was slashed or fastened by means of a sort of brooch. By the time of Henri II hats had ceased to be slashed, and the beret had made way for a flat, feather-trimmed cap (Plate 9). This afterwards became a narrow velvet toque, similarly ornamented with precious stones

15

and white feathers. It assumed an air of effeminacy at the Court of Henri III, where a more popular type of headgear was a cap with a narrow brim and a band round it, ornamented with jewels and surmounted by an *aigrette* (Plate 51).

The bulging-toed shoes of the Francis I period were supplanted in that of Henri II and Charles IX by velvet or satin pumps, covering the whole foot but slashed, and in that of Henri III by raised pattens.

Women's dress of the Francis I period is characterized by three outstanding features— the whaleboned bodice, or *vasquine*, low at the neck and often laced in front, a sort of doublet showing the wide sleeves of the chemise, and the farthingale, or stiffened petticoat widening out in the lower part, and the skirt proper, usually slit.

The Henri II period gown fitted closely at the neck (Plates 14, 18, and 39) with a small ruff or collar. The sleeves of the *vasquine* were wide on the shoulders and tight at the wrists. The *vasquine* became the quilted bodice (Plates 35, 36, 50, 51, and 52), designed to make the waist look slim, in the reign of Charles IX. The proportions of the farthingale (Plates 45, 64, 67, 68, and 70) continued to increase. Sleeves were slashed and collars pleated (Plates 8, 14, and 18).

The cambric collar developed into a ruff at the time of Catherine de' Medici (Plates 19 and 29); this consisted of a pleated frill standing up at the back of the neck and sloping towards the shoulders, held in place by a necklace called a *carcanet*. This mode was especially pronounced in the reign of Henri III (Plates 54 and 55), when the quilted bodice of the corsage, shaped like an elongated cone, imitated the peascod doublet and emphasized the fullness of the farthingale (Plate 64). Sleeves were puffed at the top and tight at the wrists, sometimes trimmed with turned-back cuffs edged with lace (Plates 52 and 54). We must also mention the vogue for 'wings' (Plates 36 and 65) attached to the shoulders and framing the nape of the neck, supported by metal under-props and made of light tissue.

Women's hair styles of the time of Francis I consisted of a *passe-filon*, or fringe of strands of hair arranged symmetrically on the forehead, or a plait kept in place at the temples by a circlet adorned with a jewel on the forehead. On their hair women wore either the bonnet-cap ornamented with pearls, supporting a veil (Plate 6), or the linen coif secured on the forehead and at the temples (Plates 19 and 30). The toque (Plate 3), which was just beginning to make its appearance, was worn chiefly at the time of Henri II, when the hair was massed and flattened down after the manner of a chignon. Under Charles IX it was drawn back from the face, the headdress being either the black velvet cap or the *escoffion* (Plate 10), a reticulated hood made of gold and silk ribbon, or else the cap with a sharp point on the forehead and terminating in a long veil hanging down the back (Plates 2, 31, and 48).

Under Henri III women's hair, instead of being stretched over pads forming rolls meeting in a point in the middle of the forehead, was dressed high on the head. A chignon was set on the nape of the neck. By way of headgear ladies affected either a conical flat-brimmed felt hat ornamented with ostrich feathers (Plate 35) or a cap with wide lappets (Plate 69).

A few minor changes had also been made in women's footgear. Under Francis I the vogue was for shoes, pumps, and pantofles made of velvet, frequently red or violet, and almost always slashed. This fashion continued under Henri II and Charles IX, but the pantofle and the pump were lower. At the time of Henri III they gave place to mules and Italian shoes, known as *pianelles* (from the word *pianella*).

We should also study the evolution of the accessories of dress, the jewellery, the furs, the *aigrettes* of feathers, the gloves, the masks, which were first worn under Charles IX, and the velvet and satin muffs, which were very fashionable at the time of Henri III. Ladies also wore at their waists a chain with a mirror or a fan dangling from it.

Our survey shows us that all through the sixteenth century there was a continuous tradition in dress, which as a whole was marked by few characteristic innovations.

We have kept to the old but still approved custom of adding a description to each plate, though illustrations are often more eloquent than commentaries, which are chiefly concerned to accentuate the outstanding features of the costumes, as the fashion journals of a later period were to do. They act as a sort of spotlight, picking out among all these pictured forms the changes in the lines and contours of the human silhouette through the ages.

NOTES ON THE ILLUSTRATIONS

PLATE 1 TITIAN: *Francis I* (Paris, Louvre).
c. 1536–39   Doublet slashed with white, scalloped standing collar with white pleated frill. Velvet cloak with a shawl collar and fur cuffs. Cap with feathers and a jewel.

PLATE 2 Attributed to FRANÇOIS CLOUET: *Marguerite of Angoulême, Queen of Navarre*
c. 1540 (sister of Francis I and author of the *Heptameron*) (Chantilly, Musée Condé).
Very simple fur-trimmed costume with a V-neck edged with pleated frilling. Cap with a veil.

PLATE 3 CORNEILLE DE LYON: *Marguerite of France* (daughter of Francis I) (Versailles Museum).
1545–50   The future Duchess of Savoy wears a sumptuous velvet gown with bands of fur ornamented with pearls. Fur collar with a pleated ruff. Necklace of precious stones with a pendant.

PLATE 4 FRANÇOIS or JEAN CLOUET: *Equestrian Portrait of Francis I* (Florence, Uffizi).
c. 1540   Sumptuous black armour, damascened with gold and finely chased, ornamented with large mascaroons. A richly caparisoned horse. Velvet toque with a feather.

PLATE 5 FRENCH SCHOOL OF THE SIXTEENTH CENTURY: *The Captain of Henri II's Escort entering*
c. 1548 *Lyon in 1548* (Paris, Department of Engravings, Louvre).
Heavily chased armour, with arm-guards and elbow-pieces. *Morion* with a flat brim and a pronounced crest, profusely trimmed with feathers.

PLATE 6 FRENCH SCHOOL OF THE SIXTEENTH CENTURY: *Claudia of France* (daughter of Louis XII
c. 1520 and wife of Francis I) (Chantilly, Musée Condé).
Narrow sleeves with lace cuffs. Matching cambric collar. Cap with a scarf. A large gold chain at the waist.

PLATE 7 Attributed to PRIMATICCIO: *Henri II* (Chantilly, Musée Condé).
c. 1547–50   Black armour damascened with silver, which can still be seen at the Musée de l'Armeé in Paris.

18

FRENCH SCHOOL OF THE SIXTEENTH CENTURY: *Catherine de' Medici, Queen of France*   PLATE 8
(Florence, Riccardi Palace).   c. 1550

The gown, of Genoese velvet, and the underskirt are trellised with pearls. Over-sleeves with a wide band of ermine. Chains of pearls and precious stones on the bodice, at the waist, and on the skirt, terminating in a pendant. Cross of precious stones at the breast. Ostrich-feather fan.

Attributed to FRANÇOIS CLOUET: *Henri II* (Paris, Louvre).   PLATE 9

Black velvet doublet and cape 'traced with gold.' Turned-over cambric collar.   c. 1559
Short, baggy trunk-hose. Toque with precious stones and feathers.

FRENCH SCHOOL OF THE SIXTEENTH CENTURY: *Diane de Poitiers* (Chantilly, Musée   PLATE 10
Condé).   c. 1550

Low-necked bodice garnished with pearls and fur. Cap with a veil.

FRENCH SCHOOL OF THE SIXTEENTH CENTURY: *A Ball in the Reign of Henri II* (Paris,   PLATE 11
Department of Engravings, Louvre).   c. 1555

Costumes of great variety, particularly as to sleeves. Bell-skirts very wide at the hem. High-necked gowns. A few floating scarfs issuing from heads or shoulders. The men wear short braided capes, with or without sleeves, with standing collars surmounted by ruffs. Very short, baggy breeches.

PERISSIN and TORTOREL: *The Death of King Henri II* (Engraving from a set of plates   PLATE 12
illustrating the wars of religion) (Paris, Department of Engravings, Louvre).   c. 1559

In the centre the doctors; on the right the Guards of the King's Chamber. Long cloaks; short slashed sleeves. Very short paned breeches.

FRENCH SCHOOL OF THE SIXTEENTH CENTURY: *Françoise, Duchess of Bouillon* (Paris,   PLATE 13
Bibliothèque Nationale).   c. 1550

Gown with a quilted bodice and a tulle yoke, and jewels. High pleated open ruff. Waved hair. A small cap with a double burlet.

FRENCH SCHOOL OF THE SIXTEENTH CENTURY: *Elizabeth of Valois* (daughter of Henri II   PLATE 14
and future Queen of Spain) (Paris, Bibliothèque Nationale).   c. 1558

Quilted bodice with a very high-necked shallow yoke. Pleated ruff, necklace of precious stones and large pearls. Hair parted in the middle. Cap of lamé tissue with precious stones.

FRENCH SCHOOL OF THE SIXTEENTH CENTURY: *Antoine de La Marck, Abbot of Beaulieu*   PLATE 15
(Paris, Bibliothèque Nationale).   c. 1550

Doublet buttoning up to the neck, with a standing collar and another turned-down collar. *Cordelières* of pearls in the form of necklaces and on the hat.

PLATE 16 Attributed to DUMONSTIER: *Francis, Duke of Guise* (Paris, Bibliothèque Nationale).
c. 1563 Doublet buttoning up to the neck surmounted by a pleated ruff. Toque with a *cordelière* and feathers.

PLATE 17 Attributed to JEAN CLOUET: *Francis I* (Paris, Louvre).
c. 1525–30 Low-necked doublet with black and white sleeves and bands of gold and silver embroidery. Hat with a white feather.

PLATE 18 FRENCH SCHOOL OF THE SIXTEENTH CENTURY: *Elizabeth of Valois* (daughter of Henri II
c. 1560 and Catherine de' Medici, wife of Philip II) (Paris, Bibliothèque Nationale).
Embroidered quilted bodice with a closely gathered tulle yoke ornamented with pearls. Pleated ruff. Sleeves with small puffs on the upper part. Diadem with jewels.

PLATE 19 SCHOOL OF CLOUET: *Madeleine de Gaignon de Saint-Bohaire* (Chantilly, Musée
c. 1560 Condé).
Chemisette with a very high pleated open ruff. Padded cap with a frill near the hair. Diadem and veil.

PLATE 20 FRENCH SCHOOL OF THE SIXTEENTH CENTURY: *Francis of France, Duke of Anjou and
c. 1560 Alençon* (fourth son of Henri II) (Paris, Bibliothèque Nationale).
Cassock with epaulettes, trimmed with *passementerie* and fur. Collar and cuffs of cambric and pleated lace. Flat, narrow-brimmed toque with pearls and feathers.

PLATE 21 FRENCH SCHOOL OF THE SIXTEENTH CENTURY: *Admiral Gaspard II de Coligny* (Paris,
c. 1560 Bibliothèque Nationale).
Rich embroidered doublet with a double collar. Flat toque with precious stones. Necklace and brooch.

PLATE 22 FRENCH SCHOOL OF THE SIXTEENTH CENTURY: *Jeanne d'Albret* (Paris, Bibliothèque
c. 1560 Nationale).
A fashion originally introduced by Catherine de' Medici. Gown with a low, square neck opening on to a *chemisette*, with large fur sleeves showing the slashed under-sleeves and a bell-shaped fur-bordered skirt. A chain of precious stones on the under-skirt. Other chains on the bodice, round the armholes, and at the waist. Necklace of uncut stones. Ruff. Diadem of pearls and a veil.

PLATE 23 FRENCH SCHOOL OF THE SIXTEENTH CENTURY: *La Damoyselle* (Paris, Bibliothèque
1560–67 Nationale).
Gown with a yoked bodice and a small ruff. Long, narrow sleeves padded on the shoulders. A bell-shaped skirt slit down the middle, suggesting a second skirt.

Attributed to CORNEILLE DE LYON: *Madame de Lansac* (Chantilly, Musée Condé). PLATE 24
A long-waisted velvet gown with a low neck opening on to a *chemisette*, with wide c. 1560
oversleeves. Cap with a diadem and a veil.

SCHOOL OF CLOUET: *Jeanne d'Albret* (daughter of Henry d'Albret and Marguerite PLATE 25
of Valois, and wife of Anthony of Bourbon) (Chantilly, Musée Condé). c. 1550
Bodice festooned with pearls. Lace yoke. Pleated open ruff. Necklace of precious
stones and pearls. A diadem and a cap.

FRANÇOIS CLOUET: *Charles IX at the Age of Eleven* (Vienna, Albertina Museum). PLATE 26
Gold-embroidered velvet doublet, edged with fur and with fur on the shoulders. 1561
Embroidered cambric collar with a pleated lace border. Velvet toque with gold braid,
pearls, and feathers.

FRANÇOIS CLOUET: *Charles IX* (Paris, Louvre). PLATE 27
Doublet with sleeves of light striped silk matching the very short breeches. Over the c. 1565
doublet a sleeveless cassock of black velvet embroidered with gold. A short cloak of
the same colour. Ruff. Lace at the wrists. Toque with precious stones and feathers.
Open slashed shoes.

Attributed to CORNEILLE DE LYON: *Madame de Canaple* (Chantilly, Musée Condé). PLATE 28
Velvet bodice with a low, square neck bordered with pearls. Puffed slashed sleeves. c. 1560–70

Attributed to FRANÇOIS CLOUET: *Jeanne d'Albret* (Chantilly, Musée Condé). PLATE 29
Bodice with a tulle yoke, and a double pleated ruff bordered with lace. The upper c. 1568–70
part of the sleeves is heavily ornamented and padded. Braids of hair intertwined
with ribbons, and a double diadem of pearls.

SCHOOL OF CLOUET: *La Baronne d'Alluye* (Versailles Museum). PLATE 30
Dark velvet bodice festooned with pearls. Paned sleeves. A white yoke with a plain c. 1565–70
upstanding collar. Cap encircled by two rows of precious stones. Necklace of white
and black pearls.

SCHOOL OF CLOUET: *Claudia de Beaune* (Paris, Petit Palais). PLATE 31
Yoked bodice garnished with pearls. Pleated open ruff. Sleeves puffed at the top. c. 1560
A very voluminous hood showing two tufts of hair.

FRENCH SCHOOL OF THE SIXTEENTH CENTURY: *Henri, Duke of Anjou* (afterwards PLATE 32
Henri III) (Paris, Department of Engravings, Louvre). c. 1570
Doublet with puffed breeches and a short cape. Ruff. A very tall, narrow-brimmed
felt hat with feathers.

21

PLATE 33 FRENCH SCHOOL OF THE SIXTEENTH CENTURY (attributed to Decourt or Jean Clouet): *The*
c. 1573 *Duke of Anjou, Dauphin of France* (Chantilly, Musée Condé).
    The inscription "Francis of France, Duke of Alençon," is incorrect. Like Henri II and Charles IX, the future Henri III wears a jerkin and short cape of dark velvet traced with gold, disclosing light-coloured sleeves and breeches. Toque with a feather.

PLATE 34 FRENCH SCHOOL OF THE SIXTEENTH CENTURY: *Duchesse de Retz* (Paris, Bibliothèque
c. 1570–75 Nationale).
    A high-necked gown, the collar turned back to show a chemisette and a ruff. A caul.

PLATE 35 FRENCH SCHOOL OF THE SIXTEENTH CENTURY: *Duchesse de Châteauneuf* (mistress of
c. 1575 Henri III) (Paris, Bibliothèque Nationale).
    Gown with revers of embroidery, enriched with metal lace. Embroidered quilted bodice with a *chemisette* and a pleated ruff. Toque with *aigrettes* and feathers.

PLATE 36 FRENCH SCHOOL OF THE SIXTEENTH CENTURY: *Elizabeth of Austria* (Paris, Bibliothèque
c. 1574 Nationale).
    Gown with a quilted bodice rising to a ruff supported by the two 'wings' of a cloak hanging behind the back and revealing very wide chequered sleeves. Skirt with a farthingale, opening on to an underskirt. Cap with feathers.

PLATE 37 GUILLAUME RICHARDIÈRE: *Henri III presiding over the First Chapter of the Order of*
c. 1578 *the Holy Spirit* (Chantilly, Musée Condé).
    Henri III, wearing the costume of the Order, a velvet stole adorned with pennants, with the Cardinals of Bourbon, Lorraine, and Birague. The Duc de Nevers, kneeling to take the oath, wears the dress of a novice of the Order, a short cloak lined with ermine, and light shoes and stockings.

PLATE 38 FRENCH SCHOOL OF THE SIXTEENTH CENTURY: *Madame de Liancourt* (Paris, Bibliothèque
c. 1579 Nationale).
    Bodice ornamented with pompons shaped like toadstools and ribbons.

PLATE 39 FRENCH SCHOOL OF THE SIXTEENTH CENTURY: *Princesse de Condé* (wife of Henri I of
c. 1575–80 Bourbon-Condé) (Paris, Bibliothèque Nationale).
    A slashed gown buttoned up to the neck. Pleated open ruff. Toque with an ostrich-feather.

PLATE 40 MARC DUVAL: *The Three Colignys* (Paris, Department of Engravings, Louvre).
1579   In the centre Admiral Gaspard de Coligny (1517–72). On his right Cardinal Odet de Coligny. On his left François de Coligny, known as Dandelot, Colonel-General of Infantry. Doublets with collars, short cloaks with sleeves, half open and ornamented with frogs. Very short puffed breeches.

FRENCH SCHOOL OF THE SIXTEENTH CENTURY: *A Peasant Girl* (Paris, Bibliothèque PLATE 41
Nationale). 1575–80
Quilted bodice laced together in front and showing the chemise with long, full
sleeves. Skirt with a farthingale and an apron. The headdress is a sort of rustic cap.

FRENCH SCHOOL OF THE SIXTEENTH CENTURY: *A Tennis-player* (Paris, Bibliothèque PLATE 42
Nationale). c. 1580
Peascod-bellied doublet, short cape, rather long breeches fastened by three buttons.
Large pleated ruff. Stockings and slippers. Feathered toque.

FRENCH SCHOOL OF THE SIXTEENTH CENTURY: *A Horseman with his Wife in the Saddle* PLATE 43
behind him (Paris, Bibliothèque Nationale). c. 1580
A masked woman in an enormous ruff, a black hood, and a bell-shaped skirt with
a farthingale. The horseman wears a peascod doublet, a cape, and a ruff.

FRENCH SCHOOL OF THE SIXTEENTH CENTURY: *A Penitent* (Paris, Bibliothèque Nationale). PLATE 44
A white penitent of the time of Henri III, barefoot and wearing a sack-like gown c. 1580
with girdle and ruff. This costume was parodied at the Salle des Cariatides.

FRENCH SCHOOL OF THE SIXTEENTH CENTURY: *A Pair of Lovers* (Paris, Bibliothèque PLATE 45
Nationale). c. 1580
Woman. A high-necked bodice with burlets on the shoulders. The skirt, with a
farthingale, shows two underskirts. Ruff. Cap with a veil. *Man.* A peascod-bellied
doublet and a ruff. Sleeves with burlets on the shoulders.

GIACOMO FRANCO: *A Dancing Couple* (Paris, Department of Engravings, Louvre). PLATE 46
An engraving from a Venetian work published in 1581 entitled *Il Ballarino*. The c. 1580
Italian dance costumes were imitated in France. Note the woman's close-fitting sleeves
with split over-sleeves. The man wears a cuirass-shaped cassock and a narrow collar.
The trunk-hose are turned up.

FRENCH SCHOOL OF THE SIXTEENTH CENTURY: *Diane de France, Duchesse d'Angoulême* PLATE 47
(Paris, Bibliothèque Nationale). c. 1580
A natural daughter of Henri II and daughter-in-law of the Constable de Montmo-
rency. A widow's cap with a hood.

Attributed to CORNEILLE DE LYON: *Presumed Portrait of Gabrielle de Rochechouart* PLATE 48
(Chantilly, Musée Condé). c. 1560–65
A low-necked gown of dark velvet with a *chemisette*. Paned sleeves puffed on
the shoulders. Small ruff.

23

PLATE 49 FRENCH SCHOOL OF THE SIXTEENTH CENTURY (attributed to QUESNEL): *Anne de Thou,*
c. 1580 *Comtesse de Cheverny* (Versailles Museum).

Open gown of dark velvet with a lace-edged Medici collar forming revers. A black
cap with white lace on the top of the head.

PLATES 50, 51 FRENCH SCHOOL OF THE SIXTEENTH CENTURY: Detail of *Ball celebrating the Marriage of*
c. 1581–82 *the Duc de Joyeuse* (Versailles Museum).

On the left (Plate 50) the Duc and Duchesse de Joyeuse. Henri III and Catherine de'
Medici are seated on the left of the Duc de Joyeuse, who wears a peascod-bellied
doublet with a ruff and long, close-fitting breeches, with stockings and flat shoes. The
Duchess's gown, with farthingale and ruff, has a double skirt and 'leg-of-mutton'
sleeves.

On the right (Plate 51) a seated woman, displaying the back of the ruff, the quilted
bodice, the puffed sleeves garnished with pearls, and the double skirt. The men, in
doublets and very long, narrow breeches, with stockings and shoes, have flat turned-
down collars or ruffs. Some wear tall felt hats with clusters of feathers. (See also
Plate 64.)

PLATE 52 FRENCH SCHOOL OF THE SIXTEENTH CENTURY: *A Ball at the Court of Henri III* (Paris,
c. 1581–82 Louvre).

In the left-hand corner Henri III, wearing a peascod-bellied doublet, tight-fitting
breeches and stockings, a turned-down collar in the Italian style, and a toque with an
aigrette. Many of the men wear pleated ruffs. All the gowns except those of the two
Queens (the King's wife and mother) have quilted bodices coming to a point below
the waist to accentuate the width of the heavily padded farthingale puffing out
the skirt.

PLATE 53 FRENCH SCHOOL OF THE SIXTEENTH CENTURY: *Marguerite of Valois* (Chantilly, Musée
c. 1570 Condé).

Daughter of Henri II and wife of Henry of Navarre. Low-necked gown with long,
narrow sleeves. Burlets on the shoulders. Quilted bodice.

PLATE 54 FLEMISH SCHOOL OF THE SIXTEENTH CENTURY: *The Fêtes of Henri III* (Florence,
c. 1580–85 Uffizi).

In the right-hand corner Henri III and Louise of Lorraine. Henri III wears a peascod-
bellied doublet with long sleeves. Cambric cuffs. Long breeches. Pleated ruff. Pearls
at the ears. Toque set very far back on the head, with jewels and feathers. Louise of
Lorraine wears an embroidered gown opening on to an embroidered underskirt. Low-
necked bodice coming to a point below the waist, with burlets on the shoulders. Long
sleeves, cambric cuffs. A lace ruff issuing from either side of the neck-opening. Headdress of pleated lace.

24

FLEMISH SCHOOL OF THE SIXTEENTH CENTURY: *The Fêtes of Henri III* (Florence, Uffizi). PLATE 55
The group on the left represents Marguerite of Valois and Henry of Navarre (Henri c. 1580–85
IV), her husband, and their brother-in-law, Charles III, Duke of Lorraine. Quilted
bodice with a low pointed neck and a ruff. Long, narrow sleeves. Skirt with embroidery at the hem, opening on to a much ornamented underskirt. *Ailerons* attached to
the upper part of the sleeves. Henry of Navarre, seen in back-view, with his head
turned showing his profile, wears a doublet and a ruff, over them a scarf and a short
cape. Long, tight-fitting breeches.

FLEMISH SCHOOL OF THE SIXTEENTH CENTURY: *The Fêtes of Henri III* (Florence, Uffizi). PLATE 56
The costume of the woman in the centre, seen in back-view, shows how the *ailerons* c. 1580–85
are attached to the burlets at the top of the sleeves. Short capes are worn by the men.
Doublets with standing collars and ruffs. Breeches reaching below the knee.

FRANÇOIS CLOUET: *Elizabeth of Austria* (wife of Charles IX) (Paris, Louvre). PLATE 57
Modes inspired by Italy. Gown of damask with a yellow ground, spangled with c. 1570–73
pearls and precious stones, with padded shoulders and paned sleeves. Ruff of
embroidery and lace. Diadem of pearls and jewels.

FRENCH SCHOOL OF THE SIXTEENTH CENTURY: *A Musketeer* (Paris, Bibliothèque PLATE 58
Nationale). c. 1585
The musket has replaced the old harquebus. Doublet surmounted by a ruff and
covered by a corslet imitating the cuirass. Wide, stiff breeches, stopping at the knee.
Felt hat with feathers.

LÉONARD GAULTIER: *Louise of Lorraine* (wife of Henri III) (Paris, Department of PLATE 59
Engravings, Louvre). 1587
A very tight-fitting bodice with slashed sleeves. Ruff with points, reaching from
the neck to the top of the head.

ITALIAN SCHOOL OF THE END OF THE SIXTEENTH CENTURY: *Feminine Silhouettes from* PLATES 60, 61
the French Provinces (Paris, Bibliothèque Nationale). c. 1580–85
Costumes of Lorraine and the districts of Vaudémont, Besançon, Orléans, and
Avignon. The Orleanese woman wears a double skirt, and the women of Lorraine
wear aprons. All wear some kind of ruff. The two Lorrainese have caps with round
brims, and the others flat caps.

HENDRIK GOLTZIUS: *The Standard-bearer* (Paris, Department of Engravings, Louvre). PLATE 62
A military costume giving an idea of the paunch, a sort of hump stuffed with horse- 1587
hair and tow, serving as a protection against bullets.

PLATE 63 FRENCH SCHOOL OF THE SIXTEENTH CENTURY: *Louise of Lorraine* (wife of Henri III)
c. 1589 (Paris, Bibliothèque Nationale).
    Low-necked quilted bodice. Lace-trimmed open ruff attached to the shoulders by
tulle. Upswept hair and a narrow veil behind the head.

PLATE 64 FRENCH SCHOOL OF THE SIXTEENTH CENTURY: Detail of *Ball celebrating the Marriage*
c. 1581–82 *of the Duc de Joyeuse* (Versailles Museum).
    A composition which should be compared with the one entitled *A Ball at the Court
of Henri III* or *The Duc d'Alençon's Ball* (Plate 52). The couple in the centre has
been wrongly identified as representing the Duc and Duchesse de Joyeuse, who are
actually standing on the King's right on the extreme left of Plate 50. The woman
has a white-and-gold gown with an unusually long quilted bodice and double sleeves.
The oversleeves, open and very long, fall almost to the bottom of the wide skirt with
a farthingale. Spreading ruff. Cap with feathers. Her partner wears a peascod-bellied
doublet with a short grey cape lined with red velvet and a pleated ruff. Tight breeches
reaching below the knee. Stockings, slippers, felt hat with feathers.

PLATE 65 PIERRE BERTELLIUS: *A French Noblewoman* (Paris, Department of Engravings, Louvre).
c. 1590   Cloak shaped at the waist and supported on the shoulders by a wire frame forming
a sort of shell, which is repeated in the skirt. The farthingale is not pronounced.

PLATE 66 PIERRE BERTELLIUS: *La Parisienne* (Paris, Department of Engravings, Louvre).
c. 1590   Gown with a quilted bodice and a plain skirt caught up at the sides and showing
a second skirt. Sleeves with mahoitres, very wide at the top and open under the arms.
Ruff issuing from the shoulders and forming a Medici collar. Flat, square cap.

PLATE 67 FRENCH SCHOOL OF THE SIXTEENTH CENTURY: *The Promenade* (Paris, Department of
End of six- Engravings, Louvre).
teenth century   A low-necked gown with slashed sleeves showing those of the cassock. Skirt with
a farthingale and underskirt. High fan-shaped ruff.

PLATE 68 FRENCH SCHOOL OF THE SIXTEENTH CENTURY: *Woman with a Fan* (Paris, Department
End of six- of Engravings, Louvre).
teenth century   Gown with a quilted bodice, the waist sharply defined by the padding of the farthingale. The front of the gown forms an apron, with two skirts showing below it.

PLATE 69 FRENCH SCHOOL OF THE SIXTEENTH CENTURY: *Damoiselles Françaises* (Paris, Depart-
End of six- ment of Engravings, Louvre).
teenth century   Low-necked black velvet gown *(left)* supported by a farthingale. Slit sleeves.
Overskirt looped up very high and draped down the sides. Fan-shaped ruff.

26

FRENCH SCHOOL OF THE SIXTEENTH CENTURY: *Five Feminine Costumes* (Paris, Department of Engravings, Louvre).

PLATE 70
End of sixteenth century

One of the gowns is caught up to form a round apron showing the underskirt. The middle figure presents the same silhouette as the other three, composed of a quilted bodice and a flat farthingale. The fifth is a servant with a cambric apron.

FRENCH SCHOOL OF THE SIXTEENTH CENTURY: *A Knight of the Holy Spirit in the Habit of his Order* (Paris, Department of Engravings, Louvre).

PLATE 71
End of sixteenth century

The knight's costume, of which the sleeves of the doublet and one side of the breeches are visible, is covered by a cloak, decorated with pennants, with an embroidered velvet train and forming a wide stole in front. The cape is studded with H's, representing the initial of Henri III, who founded the order in 1578.

BIBLIOGRAPHY

Marche, Olivier de la: *Le Parement et le triomphe des dames* (Paris, 1510).

Marche, Olivier de la: *L'Entrée triomphante et somptueuse de Madame Léonore d'Autriche, sœur ainée de l'Empereur, Royne de France, en la noble ville et cité de Paris* (1530).

Marche, Olivier de la: *Entrée de la Reyne Eléonore en la ville et cité de Bordeaux* (1530).

La Perrière, Guillaume de: *Le Théâtre des Bons Engins* (Paris, 1539).

Alciati, Andrea: *Emblematum libellus* (Paris, 1534 and 1545).

Alciati, Andrea: *La magnificence de la superbe et triomphante entrée en la noble et antique cité de Lyon, faicte au très chrétien Roy de France Henri II et à la Royne Catherine, son épouse, le 21 septembre 1548* (Lyon, 1549).

Billon, François de: *Le Fort inexpugnable de l'honneur du sexe feminin* (Paris, 1555).

Rabutin, François de: *Commentaires* (Paris, 1558).

Rabutin, François de: *Recueil de ce qui a este faict à la joyeuse et triomphante entrée du Roy Charles IX en sa bonne ville et cité de Paris, le 6 mars 1572, avec le couronnement de la très haute, très illustre et excellente princesse Elizabeth d'Autriche, son épouse* (Paris, 1572).

Rabelais, François: *Oeuvres contenant les cinq livres de la vie de Gargantua et de Pantagruel* (Lyon, 1574).

Estienne, Henri: *Dialogues du nouveau langage françois italianisé* (Paris, 1578).

Bruyn, Abraham de: *Omnis pene Europæ habitus* (Antwerp, 1581).

Boissard, Jean-Jacques: *Habitus variarum orbis gentium* (Malines, (?) 1581).

Caroso, Fabritio: *Il Ballarino* (Venice, 1581).

Beaujoyeulx, Balthazar de: *Ballet comique de la Royne, faict aux nopces de M. le duc de Joyeuse et de mademoiselle de Vaudémont, sa sœur* (Paris, 1582).

Vigenère, Blaise de: *Les Décades qui se trouvent de Tite-Live, mises en langue françoise* (Annotations; Paris, 1583).

Estienne, Antoine: *Remonstrance charitable aux dames et damoyselles de France sur leurs ornemens dissolus* (Paris, 1585).

Montaigne, Michel de: *Essais* (ed. Mlle de Gournay; Paris, 1595).

Vecellio, Cesare: *Degli habiti antichi e moderni* (Venice, 1590).

Bertellius, Pierre: *Diversarum nationum habitus* (Patavii, 1589–96).

Brantôme, Pierre de Bourdeilles, Seigneur de: *Vies des dames galantes* (Leyden, 1666).

Artus, Thomas: *Description de l'Isle des Hermaphrodites, XVIe siècle* (Cologne, 1724).

Lamarre, Nicolas de: *Traité de la police*, vol. i (Amsterdam, 1729).

Montluc, Blaise de: *Commentaires* (new edition of the work on the sixteenth century by Petitot; Paris, 1822).

Lippomano, Jérôme: *Voyage en France en 1577 (Relations des ambassadeurs vénitiens sur les affaires de France au XVIe siècle)* (extracts from the collection of original documents on the history of France; Paris, 1838).

Coquillart, Guillaume: *Contre les modes sous Louis XI* (new edition of the sermons of this fifteenth-century canon by Héricault; Paris, 1857).

Haton, Claude: *Mémoires* (sixteenth-century) (ed. Bourquelot; Paris, 1857).

Regnier de la Planche: *Histoire de l'estat de France sous le règne de François II* (new edition; Paris, 1884).

Valois, Marguerite de: *Mémoires* (sixteenth century) (ed. Bonnefon; Paris, 1920).

Menot, Michel: *Réédition de sermons des premières années du XVIe siècle* (Paris, 1924).

Plate 1   Titian   c. 1536-39

Plate 3   Corneille de Lyon   1545-50

Plate 2   Attributed to François Clouet   c. 1540

Plate 4   François or Jean Clouet   c. 1540

Plate 5   French School   c. 1548

Plate 6   French School   c. 1520

Plate 17 Attributed to Jean Clouet c. 1525-30

Plate 18   French School   c. 1560

Plate 19   School of Clouet   c. 1560

Plate 20   French School   c. 1560

Plate 21   French School   c. 1560

La Damoyſelle.

Telles on voit Françoyſes damoyſelles
En leur maintien gracieuſes & belles,
Leur entretien à tous eſt agreable,
Et pleine ſont de grace inconparable.

Plate 23   French School   1560-67

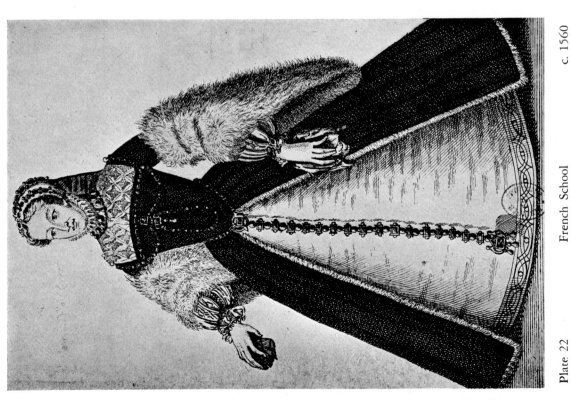

Plate 22   French School   c. 1560

Plate 24   Attributed to Corneille de Lyon   c. 1560

Jeanne   D'Albret

Plate 25   School of Clouet   c. 1550

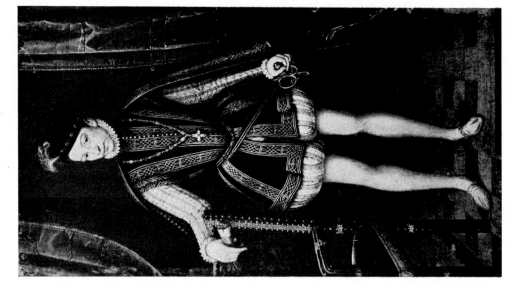

Plate 27   François Clouet   c. 1565

Plate 26   François Clouet   1561

Plate 29   Attributed to François Clouet c. 1568-70

Plate 28   Attributed to Corneille de Lyon   c. 1560-70

Plate 30   School of Clouet   c. 1565-70

Plate 31   School of Clouet   c. 1560

Plate 33　　　　　　　　French School　　　　　　　　c. 1573

Plate 32　　　　　　　　French School　　　　　　　　c. 1570

Plate 34   French School   c. 1570-75

Plate 35   French School   c. 1575

Plate 36   French School   c. 1574

Plate 37   Guillaume Richardière   c. 1578

Plate 38   French School   c. 1579   Plate 39   French School   c. 1575-80

Plate 40   Marc Duval   1579

Plate 41   French School   1575-80   Plate 42   French School   c. 1580

Plate 43   French School   c. 1580   Plate 44   French School   c. 1580

Plate 54   Flemish School   c. 1580-85

Plate 55   Flemish School   c. 1580-85

Plate 56   Flemish School   c. 1580-85

Plate 57   François Clouet   c. 1570-73

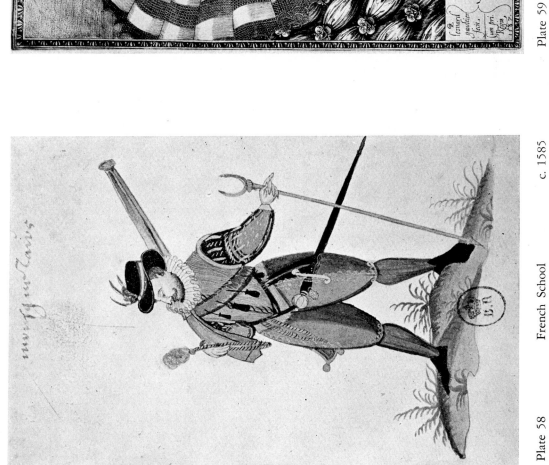

Plate 58   French School   c. 1585   Plate 59   Léonard Gaultier   1587

c. 1580-85

Italian School

Plate 60

Gentil donna de besanson.   Gentil donna d'orleans.   Gentil donna d'auignon.

Plate 61   Italian School   c. 1580-85

Plate 62　　　　　　　Hendrik Goltzius　　　　　　　1587

Plate 63　　　　　　　French School　　　　　　　c. 1589

Plate 64   French School   c. 1581

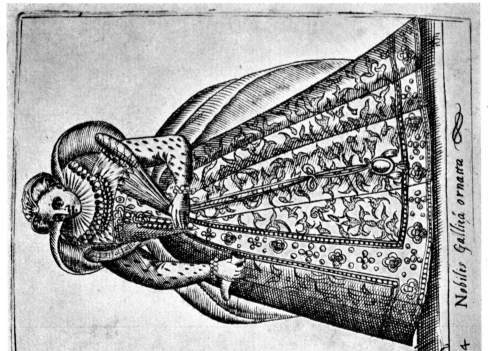

Femina Parifina ornata.

35

Plate 66   Pierre Bertellius   c. 1590

Nobilis Gallica ornatta

34

Plate 65   Pierre Bertellius   c. 1590

Plate 67   French School   end of 16th century   **Plate** 68   French School   end of 16th century

Plate 69   French School   end of 16th century

Plate 70   French School   end of 16th century

Plate 71 French School end of 16th century